Journey Around

Our

NATIONAL PARKS

Welcome to Our National Parks!

By Martha Day Zschock

Commonwealth Editions
Carlisle, Massachusetts

For the benefit and enjoyment of the people,

and for my wonderful family!

A special thank-you to my friends at
Applewood Books for their assistance
and patience with this journey.

Copyright © 2016 by Martha Day Zschock

978-1-938700-36-1

Published in cooperation with the National Park Foundation

Book design by Heather Zschock

Published by Commonwealth Editions,
an imprint of Applewood Books, Inc.,
P.O. Box 27, Carlisle, Massachusetts 01741

Visit us on the web at www.commonwealtheditions.com
Visit Martha Day Zschock on the web at www.marthazschock.com

Printed in the United States of America

10 9 8 7 6 5 4 3 2

Welcome to America's National Parks!

AMERICANS ARE LUCKY — from one coast to the other we are blessed with a treasure chest filled with the country's most spectacular natural, cultural, and historic wonders. These are our national parks!

Since 1872, forward-thinking Americans have built a vast collection of parks that preserve special places important to our heritage. Thanks to their hard work and vision, landscapes, wildlife, and memories that might have been lost forever have been saved and protected for everyone to enjoy. Each of the parks has a story to share, and together they reflect the history and spirit of our country.

The best part is that these parks belong to all Americans! Our national parks are a legacy, a gift for you and all future generations of Americans to enjoy!

Hey, kids! Ask a Ranger about how you can become a Junior Ranger and earn cool badges and certificates as you explore, learn about, and protect the parks that you visit!

Start your journey at the visitor center for maps and information about the park you are visiting. Can't go to a park today? No problem! Go to http://www.nps.gov/webrangers/ and start exploring!

OUR NATIONAL PARKS
from sea to shining sea!

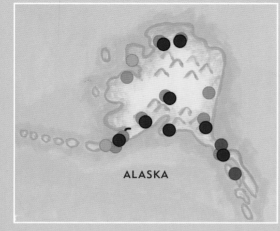

ALASKA

There are many different kinds of parks to enjoy: historic sites, memorials, monuments, battlefields, historic homes, presidential places, scenic landscapes, geological wonders, trails, shores, parkways, and more. With at least one site in every state, you're never far from a new discovery!

- ● **National Park**
- ● **National Lakeshore or Seashore**
- ● **National Monument**
- ● **National Preserve or Reserve**
- ● **National Recreation Area**
- ● **National Battlefield, Battlefield Park, Battlefield Site, or Military Park**
- ● **National Historical Park**
- ● **National and International Historic Site**
- ● **National Memorial**
- ○ **Other Designations**
- 〜 **National Parkway**
- 〜 **National Scenic Trail**
- 〜 **National River, National Wild and Scenic River and Riverway**

GUAM

HAWAII

AMERICAN SAMOA

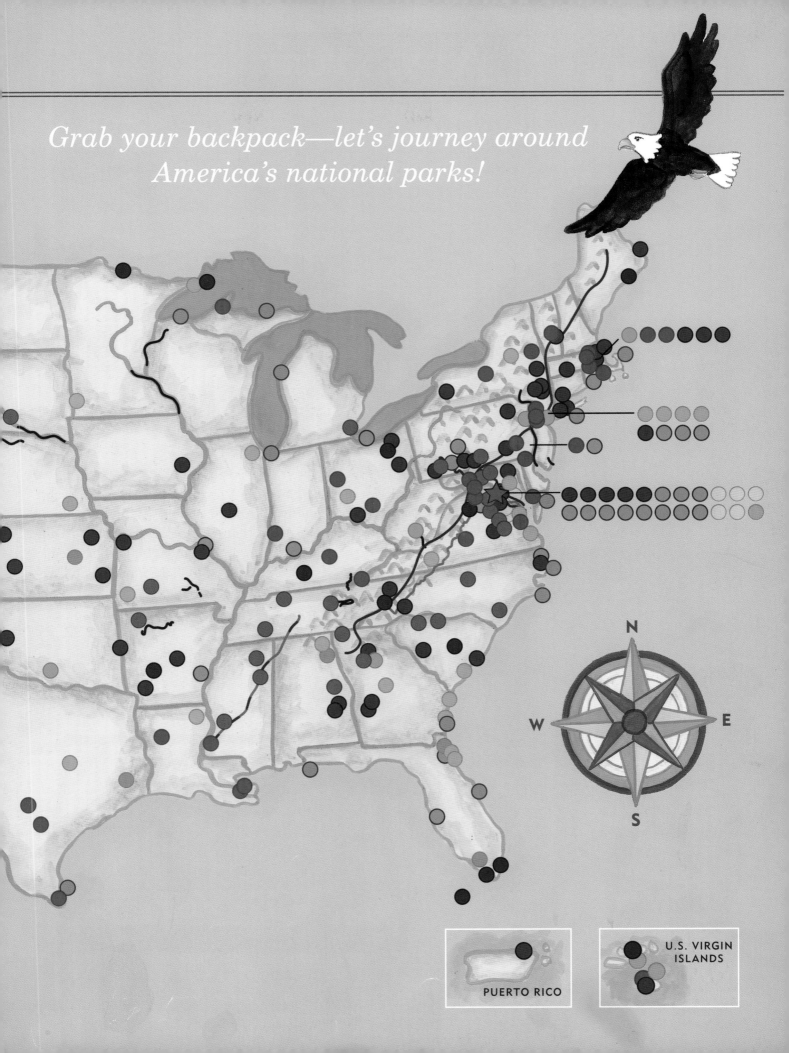

Grab your backpack—let's journey around America's national parks!

GET READY FOR ADVENTURE! America has more than 400 national parks for you to explore! Some are small and can be visited in an afternoon, while others are large and would take a lot longer. For example, several small states could fit within the borders of Alaska's Wrangell–St. Elias, our largest national park! The smallest park is Thaddeus Kosciuszko National Memorial in Pennsylvania at .02 acre. Big or small, each park preserves something special for you to discover!

> "Live in the sunshine, swim the sea,
> drink the wild air."
> —RALPH WALDO EMERSON

ZION

EVERGLADES

HOT SPRINGS

BADLANDS

YELLOWSTONE

OLYMPIC

MINUTE MAN

ADVENTURE AWAITS

Wealthy summer residents wanting to preserve the rugged beauty of Maine's Mount Desert Island donated land to create Acadia National Park. Exploring tide pools, biking on historic carriage roads, hiking, and afternoon popovers overlooking Jordan Pond are favorite activities. Bird-watchers can help collect data during the annual Hawk Watch and might even see a peregrine falcon!

ACADIA NATIONAL PARK

BIODIVERSITY

GRAND TETON NATIONAL PARK

MAMMOTH CAVE NATIONAL PARK

Our planet thrives on a rich diversity of plant and animal species and communities. We are only beginning to realize the deep connection between every bird, bear, bat, bush, and bug. From small deserts to glacier-topped mountains, our national parks preserve a wide variety of native ecosystems. Many are the last remaining ones of their kind and provide a safe haven for threatened and endangered species.

SAGUARO NATIONAL PARK

VIRGIN ISLANDS NATIONAL PARK

"When we try to pick out anything by itself, we find it hitched to everything else in the universe."
—JOHN MUIR

CULTURE

When cowboys and miners stumbled upon the magnificent Native American ruins of Mesa Verde in the late 1800s, word soon spread of their discovery. There were no laws in place to prevent the sightseers and "pot hunters" from camping in the cliff dwellings and removing important artifacts from the site. In 1906, Mesa Verde National Park became the first of its kind to celebrate a prehistoric culture and protect the "works of man."

PREHISTORIC SITES

MESA VERDE Who lived here? What was life like long ago? What happened to the people who no longer live here? Prehistoric sites leave no written records to answer such questions. Archeologists piece together the past by studying artifacts, objects, sites, and legends for clues. Petroglyphs like those found at Mesa Verde and mounds like the ones at Effigy Mounds National Monument in Iowa spark our curiosity!

EFFIGY MOUNDS

DISCOVER

There's a LOT to discover in our most-visited national park. The Great Smoky Mountains, known as the "Salamander Capital of the World," are home to an estimated 1,500 black bears and a WIDE diversity of plants, animals, and invertebrates. Scientists have identified over 17,000 species in the park and estimate that there actually may be more than twice as many living there. The park also preserves historic buildings, artifacts, and landscapes that tell the story of the diverse cultures who once called these mountains home.

GREAT SMOKY MOUNTAINS NATIONAL PARK

Mountains, glaciers, and weather laid the foundation for the wide diversity of life found in the Smokies. Many species living here have had a looonnnggg time to diversify—these mountains are over 200 million years old!

ECOSYSTEMS

Ecosystems are communities of plants and animals interacting with each other and with their home habitat. Sadly, habitat loss, climate change, overexploitation, introduction of nonnative species, development, and other threats have caused many species to suffer or disappear. As many of these factors threatened Florida's expansive Everglades, conservationists crusaded to save what they could of this unique wetland ecosystem. In 1947, Everglades National Park became the first park established to protect a large wilderness area for the benefit of the diversity of life it sustains.

"One touch of nature makes
the whole world kin."
—WILLIAM SHAKESPEARE

THE ONE AND ONLY EVERGLADES

ALLIGATOR

The Everglades ecosystem is fed by a 50-mile-wide river connecting a series of unique habitats that include sawgrass marshes, mangrove forests, hardwood hammocks, and more. The area is home to many threatened and endangered species and is the only place in the world where alligators and crocodiles live side by side!

CROCODILE

FAMILY FUN

Our national parks protect many things, including you! Having fun, learning new things, and spending time outdoors is healthy for your body and brain. Recreation areas, lakes, rivers, seashores, mountains, trails, and historic sites offer many different ways to relax and renew. Enjoy finding your favorite park and activities while spending time with your family and friends!

BUFFALO NATIONAL RIVER

**SLEEPING BEAR DUNES
NATIONAL LAKESHORE**

**PICTURED ROCKS
NATIONAL LAKESHORE**

CAPE COD NATIONAL SEASHORE

"When was the last time you did something for the first time?"
—JOHN C. MAXWELL

GEOLOGY

Glaciers, caves, canyons, volcanoes, mountains, fossil beds, petrified trees, arches, sand dunes, and more—our national parks house the most magnificent rock collections in the world! Geologic sites help us to learn about changes in our Earth over long periods of time. Geologists study these wonders to better understand earth systems, the succession and diversity of life, climate changes, the evolution of landforms, and more. Some of these formations are millions of years old!

DINOSAUR NATIONAL MONUMENT

KENAI FJORDS NATIONAL PARK

HAWAI'I VOLCANOES NATIONAL PARK

ARCHES NATIONAL PARK

BRYCE CANYON NATIONAL PARK

WIND CAVE NATIONAL PARK

PETRIFIED FOREST NATIONAL PARK

Finding interesting rocks and fossils is exciting, but help the parks to protect these and other treasures. When objects are removed, important scientific evidence is lost forever. Instead, take or draw a picture and share your discovery with a Ranger.

HISTORY

PETROGLYPH NATIONAL
MONUMENT

WOMEN'S RIGHTS
NATIONAL HISTORICAL PARK

EDGAR ALLAN POE
NATIONAL HISTORIC SITE

SAN ANTONIO MISSIONS
NATIONAL HISTORICAL PARK

SAN FRANCISCO MARITIME
NATIONAL HISTORICAL PARK

WRIGHT BROTHERS
NATIONAL MEMORIAL

Many people associate national parks with nature and wilderness, but almost two-thirds of our national parks are devoted to preserving the history of our land and its people. These sites represent a time line of American history and offer a peek into the past, connecting stories and events to physical locations. In our parks, you can discover history right where it happened!

**"The more you know
about the past,
the better prepared you
are for the future."**
—THEODORE ROOSEVELT

BOSTON NATIONAL HISTORICAL PARK

IDEA

Almost as soon as they were discovered by explorers, America's natural riches were destroyed in the name of progress. Native American cultures, wildlife, and beautiful landscapes were lost to a rapidly growing nation. Saddened by these losses, writers, poets, and artists shared the beauty of nature's wonders in their work, helping to inspire the idea for national parks—often referred to as America's "best idea"!

YOSEMITE NATIONAL PARK

Yosemite became the first area of public land set aside as protected wilderness when it was entrusted to the state of California in 1864. The valley had a great advocate in John Muir, an early conservationist who fell in love with the valley. In his descriptive writings, he urged for the area's continued protection. Yosemite later became a national park in 1890.

JOURNEY

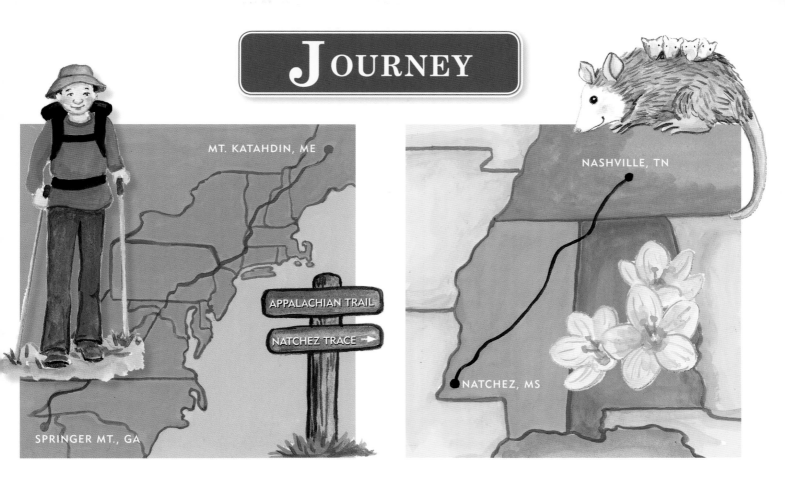

MT. KATAHDIN, ME

NASHVILLE, TN

APPALACHIAN TRAIL

NATCHEZ TRACE →

NATCHEZ, MS

SPRINGER MT., GA

Have you ever wondered what it would be like to travel through time? Our national scenic and historic trails and parkways connect historic, cultural, and natural sites along routes once traveled by glaciers, prehistoric animals, Native Americans, explorers, traders, pioneers, freedom seekers, and more. The sights, smells, and sounds connecting past to present give us an understanding of what it would have been like to walk in someone else's shoes long ago.

BLUE RIDGE PARKWAY

"The best journeys answer questions that in the beginning you didn't think to ask."
—JEFF JOHNSON

Despite President Theodore Roosevelt's urging, Congress initially failed to approve the Grand Canyon as a national park. In 1906, he signed the Antiquities Act, which granted the president the exclusive power to save important public lands as national monuments. In 1908, Roosevelt used the Act to declare the Grand Canyon a national monument in order to ensure its protection. President Carter used the Act in 1978 to ensure protection of more than 50 million acres in Alaska.

"I want to ask you to keep this great wonder of nature as it now is.... Leave it as it is. You cannot improve on it. The ages have been at work on it, and man can only mar it."

—THEODORE ROOSEVELT

AMERICA'S FIRST NATIONAL MONUMENT

Devils Tower, our first national monument, rises strikingly from the Wyoming prairie. The site is considered sacred by several Native American tribes. Native stories explain the unusual vertical marks of the tower as having been created by bears scratching their way to the top.

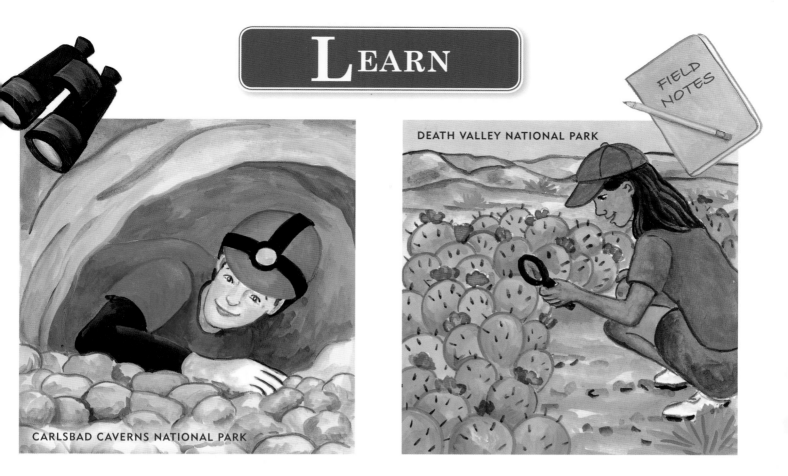

CARLSBAD CAVERNS NATIONAL PARK

DEATH VALLEY NATIONAL PARK

FIELD NOTES

Our national parks are perfect places to learn about ourselves and the world around us. They are classrooms where you can use your senses to investigate, observe, and connect to the stories and places that surround you. Oldest, tallest, deepest, longest — they fill us with a sense of wonder and teach lessons that will stay with us for a lifetime.

CRATER LAKE NATIONAL PARK

DRY TORTUGAS NATIONAL PARK

Many scientists conduct studies in our parks. Your observations and findings in the field can help scientists gather information: Use telescopes to study the night sky, investigate fossils, put on a headlamp and hard hat to explore the deepest caves, slip on snorkel gear to study coral reefs, and more. Take pictures, draw sketches, and make field notes of what you find!

MEMORIALS & MILITARY SITES

As our collection of national parks grew, the park idea expanded to include memorials and military sites. These special places help us to remember important events and defining moments in our nation's past. They remind us of the struggles and sacrifices made to defend America's founding principles of freedom, liberty, and justice for all.

"Our debt to the heroic men and valiant women in the service of our country can never be repaid. They have earned our undying gratitude. America will never forget their sacrifices."

—HARRY S. TRUMAN

LINCOLN MEMORIAL

GETTYSBURG NATIONAL MILITARY PARK

NATIONAL PARK SERVICE

On August 25, 1916, our government established a new agency to safeguard our parks. For the past hundred years, dedicated National Park Service employees and volunteers have been caring for our natural, cultural, and historic treasures, helping to educate visitors and preserve our parks for the future. As a new century dawns, the agency seeks new ways to encourage every American to connect with our parks, hoping to inspire the next generation of park stewards.

STEPHEN TYNG MATHER
1867–1930

THERE WILL NEVER COME AN END TO
THE GOOD THAT HE HAS DONE.

STEPHEN MATHER, NATIONAL PARK SERVICE'S FIRST DIRECTOR

Stephen Mather was both an enthusiastic conservationist and successful businessman. Bronze plaques at several parks honor his great contributions: "He laid the foundation of the National Park Service, defining and establishing the policies under which its areas shall be developed and conserved unimpaired for future generations."

MOUNT RAINIER NATIONAL PARK

OCEANS

Traveling on a continuous journey through oceans, rivers, lakes, streams, and the atmosphere, water connects and supports all forms of life. Despite the fact that oceans cover 70 percent of our planet, most of the underwater world is a mystery. From whales spouting off the tip of Cape Cod, Massachusetts, in the Atlantic to the coral reefs surrounding American Samoa in the Pacific, our parks conserve over 11,000 miles of coast and 2.5 million acres of ocean and Great Lakes waters. Dive in and learn about how you can help protect our water resources!

UNDERWATER ECOSYSTEMS

As on land, there are many different ecosystems underwater. Kelp forests, marshes, tide pools, coral reefs, and glacier bays all support different communities of plants and animals. Scientists use tagging to track the journeys of whales, sharks, and sea turtles as they travel through many different systems. The research gathered helps teach us how to better understand and protect these animals.

"The sea, once it casts its spell, holds one in its net of wonder forever."
—JACQUES COUSTEAU

PRESERVE & PROTECT

When the National Park Service was established, there was little understanding of the interconnectedness between all living things and their environment. Management focused on individual park features: Fires were suppressed to protect giant trees, bears were fed, and predators removed. These decisions were popular with tourists but disrupted the delicate balance of nature, hurting the very treasures they were trying to protect. Scientific study has led to better care—now complete environments are protected and visitors are taught to interact with and appreciate nature without disturbing it.

BEAR SAFETY

Bears and other wildlife are wild, and it is best for you, and them, to keep it that way! Interacting with them can lead to dangerous encounters. Follow directions for storing food and garbage properly, and learn more about what you can do to help the National Park Service keep our parks truly "unimpaired" for future generations.

FOOD STORAGE

Sequoia trees can live to be over 3,000 years old! How did these giants get to be so old? In part, the answer is due to naturally occurring cycles of forest fire. After a century of suppressing fires, park scientists began to notice that there were no new saplings. They began experimenting with controlled burns and studied the growth rings of fallen trees for fire scars. Their findings showed that fire was an essential process that kept sequoias and the surrounding forest healthy.

FOREST FIRES

Fires help sequoias in many ways: Flames open cones, clear the ground, fertilize the soil, and open up areas to allow sunlight and moisture to reach the saplings. When underbrush isn't cleared regularly by small fires, it can build up and lead to massive wildfires if ignited.

RANGER

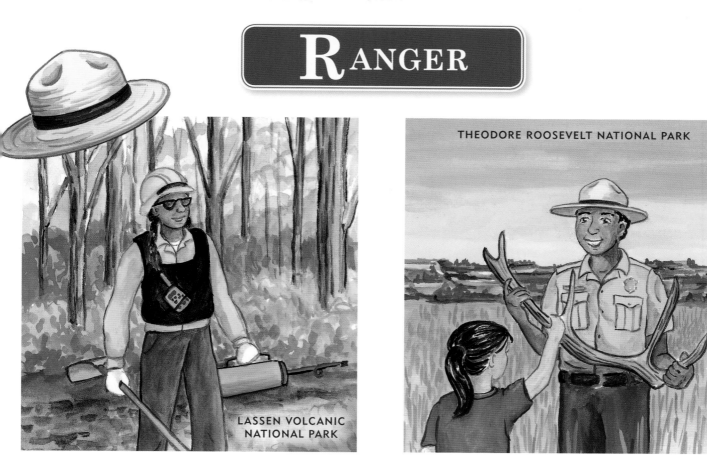

THEODORE ROOSEVELT NATIONAL PARK

LASSEN VOLCANIC NATIONAL PARK

Have a question, need a map, looking for help? Ask a Ranger! National Park Service Rangers play many different roles as stewards of our natural, cultural, and historic treasures, helping to make your park experience fun, educational, and enjoyable. Rangers help with interpretation, education, management, administration, law enforcement, firefighting, wildlife care, carpentry, mechanics, scientific research, and rescue missions—and they wear really cool hats!

ROCKY MOUNTAIN NATIONAL PARK

PADRE ISLAND NATIONAL SEASHORE

Attitudes and beliefs change with the times, and the National Park Service is no different. Women were prevented from holding Ranger jobs equal to men's until 1971 and couldn't wear the same uniform, badge, and really cool hat until 1978!

1962

1970

SYMBOLS OF AMERICA

WASHINGTON MONUMENT

INDEPENDENCE NATIONAL HISTORICAL PARK

The idea for national parks—that our most treasured places be protected for everyone to share and enjoy—is a uniquely democratic, American idea. The park system as a whole has come to represent the spirit of America, encompassing our stories, struggles, and fights to uphold our founding principles of freedom, justice, and liberty for all. Many sites are recognized around the world as symbols of our country and its ideals.

MOUNT RUSHMORE NATIONAL MEMORIAL

HELLO, PRESIDENT!

The colossal carved faces of four famous presidents (Washington, Jefferson, Lincoln, and Theodore Roosevelt), gaze down on visitors from Mount Rushmore National Memorial, a symbol of hope and freedom. This memorial invites visitors to learn about the birth, growth, development, and preservation of our country and celebrates the diversity of the American people, connecting us through our shared heritage.

TRIUMPH & TRAGEDY

TRAIL OF TEARS NATIONAL HISTORIC TRAIL

WHITE   COLORED

BROWN V. BOARD OF EDUCATION NATIONAL HISTORIC SITE

MANZANAR NATIONAL HISTORIC SITE

Traditionally, the retelling of history has led to one-sided accounts of the past. Our national parks strive to accurately represent all sides of our diverse American story and to include the experiences of all Americans. Triumphs and tragedies, glory and remorse are displayed side by side so that we may learn from our mistakes, celebrate our successes, and face the future with a deeper understanding and appreciation for each other and our shared heritage.

"To communicate the truths of history is an act of hope for the future."
—DAISAKU IKEDA

STATUE OF LIBERTY NATIONAL MONUMENT

URBAN ESCAPES

Many of our national park sites are located in the middle of our country's busiest cities. More than 80 percent of Americans live in urban areas, and these parks allow city folks an escape from the hustle and bustle of daily life. Bike trails, paths, fields, historic sites, and waterways offer a chance to relax and have fun outdoors without going far from home.

URBAN SITES

The National Park Service continually strives to find ways to encourage Americans to discover their parks. Collaborations within communities and neighborhoods help to bring our parks closer to every American.

GATEWAY NATIONAL RECREATION AREA

VISITORS

Long ago, most people could only read about and imagine the beauty to be found in our first national parks. Railroads promoted these early parks to increase their business and built grand "rustic" hotels to entice wealthy travelers accustomed to traveling abroad. Poster campaigns encouraged visitors to "See America First!" In time, travel became easier and more affordable, and the number and types of parks grew, increasing accessibility. Today, our parks attract over 300 million visitors a year from all over the world!

MISSION 66

The National Park Service wasn't prepared for the large number of visitors who packed up their automobiles and headed to the parks following World War II. In 1955, they launched a massive program for park improvements to be completed by the service's fiftieth anniversary in 1966. One hundred new visitor centers were built during this time!

GLACIER NATIONAL PARK

WILDERNESS

In the early 1800s, forests, rivers, prairies, and mountains stretched westward as far as the eye could see. Americans saw opportunity in this vast, "endless" frontier and raced to expand the nation from one coast to the other. In less than a century, over half of the hardwood forests and almost all of the wild prairies were gone. Over the next century, we witnessed the far-reaching consequences of this rapid development and realized the need to preserve rather than consume our resources.

WOLVES AND WILDERNESS

The Wilderness Act, signed in 1964, preserves large undeveloped areas where "man himself is a visitor who does not remain." Wolf packs once roamed from the Arctic to Mexico. As their natural habitats were developed, they became a threat to human safety and were eliminated. By 1960, wolves were on the brink of extinction. In 1995, they were successfully reintroduced to Yellowstone and have continued to make a comeback.

EXPANSION

During the great westward expansion, millions of people left their homes and headed west in pursuit of the "American Dream." Native American cultures and natural landscapes gave way to development, diverse settlements, agriculture, and industrial advancements that built the nation and changed the land forever. Our parks preserve the adventurous spirit of early western explorers, brave pioneers, industrious inventors, and others who played a role in transforming our country.

JEFFERSON NATIONAL EXPANSION MEMORIAL

GO WEST!

Imagine packing up all of your belongings into a wagon and heading west to a new life in a small cabin on the prairie! The Gateway Arch soaring at the Jefferson National Expansion Memorial is a tribute to this time in history. Learn about the westward movement, explore pioneer life at Homestead National Monument of America and see the few remaining acres of native prairie.

HOMESTEAD NATIONAL MONUMENT OF AMERICA

Yellowstone

Boiling mud, steaming hot springs, water shooting straight up from the ground?! The first reports of Yellowstone's unusual geothermal features in the remote western frontier were thought to be fiction, and no one would publish such nonsense. When they were found to be true, preservationists encouraged the government to protect these wonders before they were lost forever. In 1872, Congress established Yellowstone, the world's first national park, "for the benefit and enjoyment of the people."

GEOTHERMAL WONDERS

Yellowstone National Park has more than 10,000 geothermal wonders, including geysers, mud pots, and hot springs, which are fueled by an active volcano lying beneath the park. Geologists use seismograph technology to monitor conditions, and they predict that the odds of a major eruption occurring anytime soon are very, very small.

Zzzzz

Starry skies and natural darkness are not often thought of as resources in need of protection, but they are! Many wildlife species rely on nocturnal habitats that are disrupted by unnatural light. Gazing at the undisturbed night sky over Zion National Park, it's easy to understand why Mormon pioneers named this special place Zion, a place of peace and refuge.

"For my part I know nothing with any certainty, but the sight of the stars makes me dream."
—VINCENT VAN GOGH

SWEET DREAMS

The fascinating sights and sounds you'll experience in our parks will make for rich dreams. While our national parks collectively tell the story of our shared heritage, your own experiences in the parks will become stories and memories to share with your family and friends. Treasure your times in the parks and help to keep them as they are. Enjoy!

ZION NATIONAL PARK

A PROMISE TO THE FUTURE

America's national parks have grown beyond the wildest dreams of early visionaries. The idea has expanded beyond park borders to influence the protection of natural and cultural resources and treasures in local communities and throughout the world. Our parks are an ever-evolving work in progress, a forever mission to preserve our past and help guide us toward the future. Now, the responsibility is ours: The future of our parks depends on all of us! Working together, we can help make America's "best idea" even better!

JUNIOR RANGER PLEDGE

"As a Junior Ranger, I promise to teach others about what I learned today, explore other parks and historic sites, and help preserve and protect these places so future generations can enjoy them."

*"The land belongs to the future…
that's the way it seems to me…
We come and go, but the land is
always here. And the people who love
it and understand it are the people
who own it—for a little while."*

—WILLA CATHER

1776
United States Declaration of Independence

1800
Millions of bison roam the plains of North America.

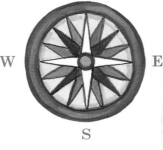

1848
Gold is discovered in California! The race is on!

1862
Homestead Act: Promises of free land entice settlers to western lands.

1861–1865
The Civil War

1863
President Lincoln signs the Emancipation Proclamation, freeing slaves in Southern states fighting against the Union.

1872
Congress establishes Yellowstone, our first national park.

1876
Battle of the Little Bighorn

1916
National Park Service established.

1920
Women gain the right to vote.

National park visitors exceed one million.

1926
Last wolves disappear from Yellowstone.

1935
Sir Arthur George Tansley introduces the concept of the "ecosystem" into biology.

1939–1945
World War II

1963
Martin Luther King Jr. gives his "I Have a Dream" speech at the Lincoln Memorial.

1969
Neil Armstrong becomes the first man to walk on the moon.

1973
Endangered Species Act signed.

1985
The word "biodiversity" is first used.

1995
Wolves are reintroduced to Yellowstone.

2001
9/11 terrorist attacks

1804
Lewis and Clark Expedition departs to explore and chart the West.

1830
Indian Removal Act

1838
Trail of Tears: Thousands of Native Americans are forced to leave their homeland.

1841
Oregon Trail: Families follow the trail to a new life in the West.

1864
The Yosemite Grant Act signed by President Lincoln grants Yosemite to the state of California for public use.

1869
The Golden Spike is laid to celebrate the completion of the first transcontinental railroad.

1890
U.S. government announces that the West has been explored.

Bison near extinction.

Yosemite becomes a national park.

1903
First flight

1906
Antiquities Act signed, allowing the president to protect special places as national monuments.

1914–1918
World War I

1929
The Great Depression: Over 13 million people lose their jobs during this period.

1933
The Civilian Conservation Corps creates new jobs.

Military parks, battlefields, monuments, and nonmilitary historical sites are put under the care of the National Park Service.

1950
National park visitors exceed 32 million.

1950–1953
Korean War

1961–1975
U.S. involvement in Vietnam

1956
Mission 66: A 10-year federal program launched by the National Park Service to improve park conditions. The concept of "visitor centers" is born!

2016
100th anniversary of the National Park Service—411 sites now!

2016 and Beyond
Our national parks are our legacy; Help to protect our parks for future generations to enjoy!

"Life is a great adventure…
accept it in such a spirit."

—THEODORE ROOSEVELT